Little Books of Nouns

by Babs Bell Hajdusiewicz

Illustrated by George Ulrich

Good Year Books
Parsippany, New Jersey

Good Year Books
are available for most basic curriculum subjects plus many enrichment areas. For more Good Year Books, contact your local bookseller or educational dealer. For a complete catalog with information about other Good Year Books, please contact:

Good Year Books
An imprint of Pearson Learning
299 Jefferson Road, P.O. Box 480
Parsippany, NJ 07054-0480

www.pearsonlearning.com

1-800-321-3106

Cover and Interior Illustrations: George Ulrich
Book Design: M. Jane Heelan
Design Manager: M. Jane Heelan
Editorial Manager: Christine Kiel
Executive Editor: Judith Adams
Production/Manufacturing Director: Janet Yearian
Senior Production/Manufacturing Coordinator: Roxanne Knoll

ISBN 0-673-59246-4

2 3 4 5 6 7 8 9 - ML - 06 05 04 03 02 01

Good Year Books

This Book Is Printed On Recycled Paper

Table of Contents

Introduction

Naming words, or nouns, are among the first words that hold meaning for infants and are among the first words toddlers speak. That's because family members often *isolate, emphasize,* and *repeat* important content words that carry meaning in a spoken sentence. Family members also tend to model, or demonstrate, the meanings of the words they speak; that is, they point to a person or object while saying the person's or thing's name. Young listeners and talkers come to understand and repeat those nouns in their eagerness to talk about the meaningful people, places, and things they encounter in daily living.

Little Books of Nouns, like its companion *Little Books of Verbs,* presents important content words in print in a way that is similar to how children experience important words in oral language. *Little Books of Nouns* contains 14 reproducible, take-home little books that invite children to have oral and print experiences with nouns in meaningful contexts. The little book stories, told in simple rhyming phrases and sentences that emphasize nouns, include lively illustrations that help to demonstrate the meanings of nouns.

The teaching suggestions that accompany the little books will help you give your young talkers and readers a meaningful and successful first introduction to nouns in print. These suggestions are organized into the following sections:

Introducing Nouns

Four introductory rhymes and several accompanying activities introduce the concept of nouns. The rhymes invite children to talk, sing, and read about nouns and what nouns do. The rhymes also act as mnemonic devices that children can "carry" with them for ongoing use in identifying nouns.

Using the Little Books

This section helps you prepare and assemble the little books. It also provides suggestions for introducing and personalizing the little books.

Making and Using Word Cards

Here you will find suggestions for using the reproducible word cards that correspond to the nouns in each of the little book stories.

Family Involvement

This section emphasizes the importance of family involvement and summarizes the content of the letters to family members.

Extension Activities

The activities suggested here provide opportunities to extend children's listening, speaking, reading, and writing experiences with nouns. While some activities focus on phonological awareness and oral language skills helpful to emerging and developing readers, other suggestions offer activities that challenge children to identify singular and plural nouns and to write original little books and poems.

Introducing Nouns

Introductory Rhymes

The following four rhymes and several accompanying activities will help you introduce the concept of nouns as naming words. Periodically, you may want to begin and end a little book with one or more of the introductory rhymes to focus children's attention on the nouns in a little book.

You can either prepare each rhyme as a chart in advance or create a chart as a shared writing activity.

Ask, "What's a noun?" and read a rhyme. Repeat the question and the poetic answer, pausing for children to point to an actual person, place, or thing, or to complete individual lines. Help children list more nouns that name people, places, and things around them. Point out that each naming word in the list is called a *noun.*

Sing the introductory rhymes "Nouns Name People," "Nouns Name Places," and "Nouns Name Things" to the tune of "Twinkle, Twinkle, Little Star." See the accompanying activities for these rhymes on the next page.

What's a Noun?

A noun names
a PERSON,
or a PLACE,
or a THING.
So my **name** is a noun.
So is **school.**
So is **ring.**
And my **city** is a noun.
It's the PLACE where I live.
And a **present** is a noun.
It's a THING that I give.

Nouns Name People

Nouns are words I use to say
the names of people every day.
my **mom**
my **aunt**
my **sister Jill**
my **dad**
my **friend**
my **Uncle Bill**
Nouns are words I use to say
the names of people every day.

Nouns Name Places

Nouns are words I use to say
the names of places every day.

backyard

playground

classroom

hall

office

lunchroom

street

and **wall**

Nouns are words I use to say
the names of places every day.

Nouns Name Things

Nouns are words I use to say the
names of things I see each day.

bus

and **car**

and **books**

and **clothes**

spoon

and **fork**

and **eyes**

and **nose**

Nouns are words I use to say the
names of things I see each day.

Activities for Introductory Rhymes

- Reread "Nouns Name People." Talk about how each person has a special name. Begin a list titled "People" and invite children to say their names and others' names as you record each name. Point out your use of a capital letter to begin each person's name.
- Provide sticky notes for children to write their own or others' names to be substituted for the names in the "Nouns Name People" rhyme.
- Adapt the activities for "Nouns Name People" to use with "Nouns Name Places" and "Nouns Name Things." Help children name special things or places, such as street names, city names, or places in their neighborhoods. Emphasize the use of a capital letter to begin a proper noun that names a specific street, city, or place.

Using the Little Books

The reproducible little books may be used in any order to complement your lessons or themes. Since the use of a little book may extend over several days to a week or more, you will want to continue to Focus Talk™ around a little book to ensure that children retain and use the book's language and ideas in their daily living. (See Extension Activities: Focusing Talk™ on page 9.)

Preparing the Little Books

Each little book contains eight pages of text plus a front and back cover and inside front and back covers. The pages are arranged in this book such that you may copy one little book at a time by copying its three double-sided pages.

To make a little book for each child, cut the pages in half, collate them in order, and staple along the left side. Children will enjoy helping to assemble their books.

Introducing the Little Books

- To introduce a little book, discuss the story and illustrations. Help children relate the story to their own experiences.

- You may want to review "What's a Noun?" or one of the other introductory rhymes to help children focus on the nouns in a book.

- Ask children to listen for names of people, places, or things as you read a little book aloud. Invite children to join in during successive readings.

- Reread the story to have children identify each noun and tell what it names. List the nouns on chart paper.

- Choose from the Extension Activities which begin on page 9 to extend learning with a particular little book or to provide additional listening, speaking, reading, or writing practice with nouns.

Personalizing the Little Books

Have children write their names and the date on the inside front cover of each little book. You might model personalizing the story by saying, "This story makes me think of a time when . . . ." Invite children to complete the sentence or activity on the inside back cover of each little book.

Encourage children to read their little books to classmates and either record the listeners' names or have each listener sign on the back cover.

Making and Using the Word Cards

At the back of this book, you will find blackline masters to assist you in making a set of word cards that corresponds to the nouns in each little book's story. When you are ready to use the cards, copy the page and cut apart the cards. Some stories use the same noun several times. Make additional word cards as needed when this occurs.

The following activity suggestions may be used in lessons or in activity centers. You may want to prepare a set of word cards for each child to take home and enjoy with family members.

- Match a word card to its word in the story.
- Scramble the word cards. Then read or recite the story to place the word cards in the order the nouns appear.
- Match the rhyming nouns.
- Count the letters in words to sort the nouns by length.
- Scramble two sets of word cards for a particular story. Then match each noun to its mate. Finally, separate the cards into two sets.
- Match magnetic letters or letter cards to the letters in a word.
- Display the noun word cards under a heading such as "Nouns Name People," "Nouns Name Places," or "Nouns Name Things." Children may want to illustrate each noun.

Family Involvement

Encourage children to take home their little books to reread alone or with family members. Remind children to record listeners' names on the back cover.

Beginning on page 12, you will find three sample letters that foster family involvement in children's literacy journeys by: providing encouragement, offering suggestions for literacy activities at home, modeling literacy opportunities, and sharing information about good reading habits. You may want to have the letters translated for non-English-speaking family members.

Extension Activities

The following activities may be used with any of the little books. Many of the activities are well-suited for use in learning centers.

Dramatizing a Little Book's Story

Invite volunteers to pantomime a story from a little book, such as *My Jobs, A Party,* or *My Plants,* for classmates to guess the book's title.

Focusing Talk™

Focusing Talk around familiar literature during conversation with children models the use of "book talk" in daily living. Focused talking occurs every time you quote words from a book, innovate on a book's text, or compare an idea to a book's words or ideas.

You will find many opportunities to Focus Talk around the language of familiar little book stories. For example, a child's image in a mirror might prompt you to say, *You have two eyes. You have one nose,* . . . and so on as an innovation on the little book titled *My Body*. Or when trying to keep something from falling, you might use a metaphor or a simile while referring to the book titled *The Circus: I'm a juggler* or *I'm like a juggler in a circus.*

Identifying Rhyming Words

- Point out rhyming nouns, such as *ants/plants, weeds/seeds, hall/wall, cats/hats, door/floor,* or *cheese/peas* in a little book's story.

- Write a rhyming couplet, such as the example below, on the chalkboard or on chart paper. Encourage children to emphasize the rhyming words as they chant the couplet in unison.

> I see some plants.
>
> And I see ants!

Help children substitute other pairs of rhyming nouns to create original couplets.

Recording Read-Alouds

Invite children to record the reading of a little book and then take home the tape to enjoy alone or with family members.

Retelling a Little Book's Story

Help children retell a little book's story to include more details about each illustration. Children might retell the little book *My Jobs* by saying: *I'm a baker baking a cake; I'm a typist typing a letter; I'm an artist painting a picture* . . . . Children may want to substitute *We* or their own names and friends' names for *I*.

Help children write their retellings to create a collection of retold stories. Or help children publish their retold stories in little book format: Cover the text of a little book *before* copying the book; write or type children's words and cut them into sentence strips; match a sentence strip to each illustration in the little book and glue in place.

Writing a Story as a Poem

Use an overhead projector and transparency as you help children rewrite a little book's story in poem format. Have children read in unison a familiar little book as you or a volunteer writes the text. Some children may want to help with the placement of capital letters and punctuation. Point out how each new page in the book signals the start of a new line of the poem.

Talk about how the little book's words now appear as a poem. Make a copy for each child. As suggested in a similar activity on page 6, help children use sticky notes to innovate on the poem's text and write or type the new poems to publish an original collection.

Innovating on Texts

Encourage children to innovate on a little book's text by identifying particular nouns in a story and listing other nouns that could be used to tell the same story. For example, *I See Words* might tell about seeing words on signs, labels, computer or TV screens, or T-shirts. Help children use their noun suggestions to tell or write rhymed or unrhymed stories.

Help children change the setting of a little book's story. For example, *At School* might be changed to *At Home* or *In My Room*. Ask children what nouns would be needed to name things in these settings, and what nouns should be included in their stories.

Categorizing Nouns

Help children identify and then categorize nouns from several familiar little books to create a display in the classroom or to make a dictionary of nouns. Encourage children to add to the list as they encounter nouns while reading, watching television, or conversing.

Children might group nouns under headings such as "Nouns Name People," "Nouns Name Places," or "Nouns Name Things." Children also might organize nouns by beginning letter, by the number of letters in a word, or by topic, such as "Animals," "Cities Around Us," or "Our Favorite Fruits." Using word cards for nouns, this activity works well in a learning center.

Nouns That Begin with P	
pan	paper
pizza	pickle

Writing Original Little Books and Poems

Help children brainstorm lists of nouns around specific topics, such as "Tools" or "Space." For example, the nouns hammer, scissors, fork, pencil, brush, and comb might be listed under "Tools." Help children use a word list to write an original rhymed or unrhymed little book or poem, such as the following:

> I see the moon.
> I see the stars.
> I see the clouds.
> I don't see Mars!

Identifying Singular and Plural Nouns

Using a familiar little book, point out a noun in the story that names one person, place, or thing. Help children identify and list other singular nouns in the story. Encourage children to add to their list as they read other books or hear nouns used in conversation. Group the nouns under the heading "Nouns That Name One."

Repeat the activity using a familiar little book, such as *At School* or *The Circus,* that includes plural nouns. List plural nouns under the heading "Nouns That Name More Than One."

Challenge: Spelling Some Plural Nouns

- Explain that *-es* is added to words that end in *ch, sh,* or *x* to name more than one. Write *s* and *es* on separate sticky notes and help children add the appropriate ending to change singular nouns to their plural forms: *book/books, pea/peas, cat/cats,* or *box/boxes, fox/foxes, peach/peaches, watch/watches, wish/wishes,* and *dish/dishes.*

- Write *fly* and tell children that the plural form of a noun that ends in *y* is spelled differently. Model changing *y* to *i* by writing *i* on a sticky note and placing it over the *y* in the word. Then add an *es* sticky note. Say the word aloud, spell the word, and say the word again. Help children change other singular nouns, such as *baby, pony, sky, penny,* or *french fry* to their plural forms (*babies, ponies, skies, pennies, french fries*).

Date:

Dear Family Members,

Do you remember your child's first words? Chances are, those words included nouns that named people, places, or things. Saying nouns, like *dad, mom,* or *bus*, is an important first step in learning to read.

Your child will be bringing home little books that focus on nouns. Your child can keep these books and read them alone or with you. You'll want to respond to your child's questions and comments about a story and praise every attempt to recognize the story's printed words.

As you read and reread each little book with your child, encourage good reading habits by:

- Using the pictures and rhyming words as clues to recognize difficult words.
- Talking about the story and relating it to your child's and your own experiences.
- Using the book's ideas and words in your conversations.
- Pointing out the use of nouns in daily conversations.

Have fun reading together!

Sincerely,

Date:

Dear Family Members,

I know that you and your child are enjoying reading these little books of nouns together at home. Although your child has read each little book of nouns several times at school, some of the words may not be remembered exactly.

Your child will learn to recognize a difficult word and enjoy "talking time" as you do the following activity:

> Write a word, such as *playground,* on four sticky notes or scraps of paper. Attach the "word notes" in the appropriate places as you say the following rhyme:
>
> *Playground* is on the window.
> *Playground* is on the floor.
> *Playground* is on the table.
> *Playground* is on the door.
>
> Repeat the rhyme, changing *on* to *off* as one of you removes each note.

Play this word game as long as your child shows interest and is having fun.

Sincerely,

Date:

Dear Family Members,

Your child has now read several little books of nouns. These books are helping your child read words that name people, places, or things.

Your child may want to read a favorite little book again and again. That's good! Here are some reasons why:

- Your child likes the story's ideas, pictures, and the sounds of the words.
- Your child likes reading a book whose words and pictures are familiar.
- Your child wants to "own" the little book's story—to use those very words and ideas in daily living.
- Your child likes the good feeling of successfully reading the little book.

And each new reading gives your child added practice in hearing and saying nouns and seeing those words in print.

Have fun pointing out nouns as you read and talk together!

Sincerely,

My Body

I have ten fingers.

2

This book belongs to

______________________________.

Today is ____________________.

8

I have ten toes.

I have two legs.

I have two knees.

I have two lips.

I have one nose.

I have two hands.

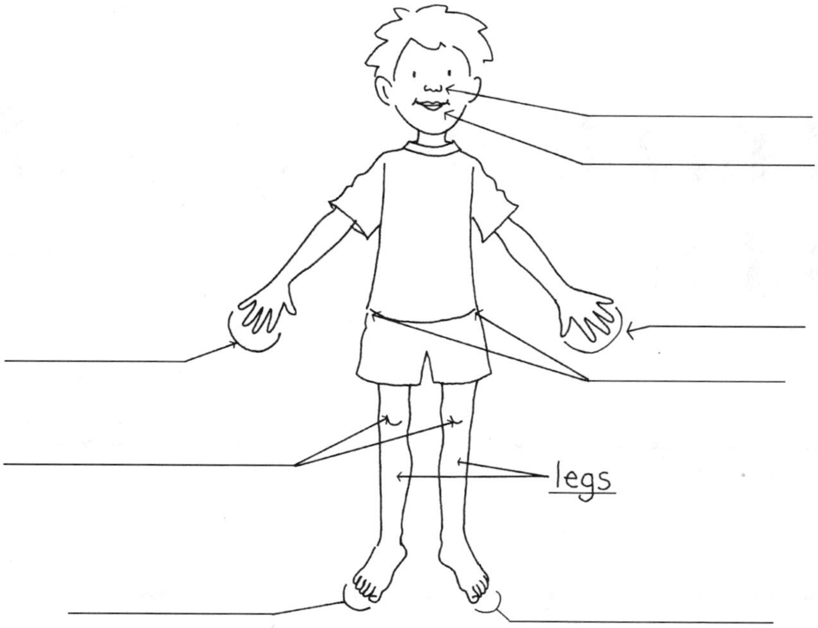

Write the nouns.

6

I have two hips.

12

I read my little book of nouns to:

1. ______________________________

2. ______________________________

3. ______________________________

Places I Like

I like the movies.

Text Copyright © Babs Bell Hajdusiewicz

2

This book belongs to

______________________.

Today is ______________.

8

I like the stores.

I like the park.

I like the playground.

4

I like the zoo.

10

I like the outdoors!

I like the circus.

I like the ________________ .

6

My sister does, too!

12

I read my little book of nouns to:

1. ______________________________

2. ______________________________

3. ______________________________

Things I Like

I like flowers.

2

This book belongs to

______________________________.

Today is ________________.

8

I like cars.

3

I like checkers.

9

I like stories.

Text Copyright © Babs Bell Hajdusiewicz

4

I like cats.

10

I like stars.

I like soccer.

I like ________________________.

6

I like hats.

12

I read my little book of nouns to:

1. ______________________

2. ______________________

3. ______________________

Lunch

7

I have pretzels.

Text Copyright © Babs Bell Hajdusiewicz

2

This book belongs to

________________________________.

Today is ____________________.

8

You have peas.

3

I have tacos.

9

I have carrots.

4

You have beans.

10

We have cheese!

I have crackers.

I have __________ for lunch.

6

You have greens.

12

I read my little book of nouns to:

1. ______________________

2. ______________________

3. ______________________

The Circus

I see acrobats.

2

This book belongs to

______________________.

Today is ______________.

8

I see clowns.

I see elephants.

I see lions.

4

I see seals.

10

I see frowns!

I see jugglers.

I see ________________ at the circus.

6

I see wheels.

12

I read my little book of nouns to:

1. ______________________

2. ______________________

3. ______________________

My Jobs

I'm an artist.

(I am)

2

This book belongs to

______________________________.

Today is ________________.

8

I'm a teacher.

I'm a bāker.

I'm a student.

4

I'm a typist.

10

I do work.

I'm a painter.

I'm a ________________________.

This is my work.

6

I'm a clerk.

12

I read my little book of nouns to:

1. ____________________

2. ____________________

3. ____________________

A Party

I write a card.

2

This book belongs to

______________________________.

Today is ______________________.

8

I see the place.

I read a day.

I knock on the door.

4

I read a name.

10

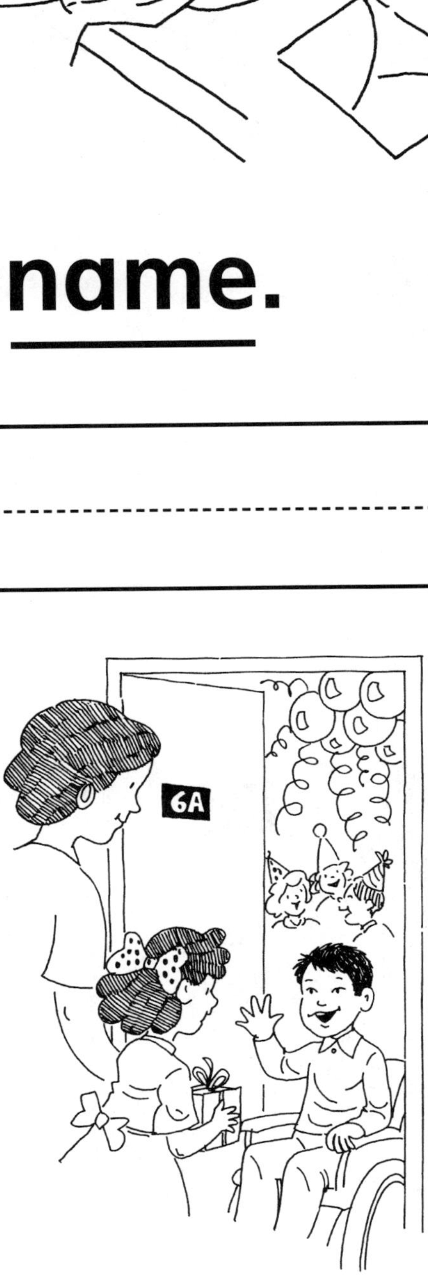

I see a face!

I read a time.
______

______ had a party.

I saw a ______ .

6

I wrap a game.

12

I read my little book of nouns to:

1. ____________________

2. ____________________

3. ____________________

At School

We use markers.

Text Copyright © Babs Bell Hajdusiewicz

2

This book belongs to

______________________________________.

Today is ____________________________.

8

We use crayons.

We use pencils.

We make posters.

4

We use paper.

10

We get cheers!

We make noses.

We use ________ at school.

We make ears.

I read my little book of nouns to:

1. ______________________

2. ______________________

3. ______________________

A Pet

Will I get a <u>hippo</u>?

2

This book belongs to

________________________________.

Today is ____________________.

8

Will I get a bat?

Will I get a hamster?

Will I get a lion?

Will I get a frog?

I will get a cat!

Will I get a turtle?

Will I get a ______________?

6

Will I get a dog?

12

I read my little book of nouns to:

1. ______________________

2. ______________________

3. ______________________

My Plants

I get some water.

2

This book belongs to

______________________________.

Today is ____________________.

8

I see some ants!

I see some dirt.

I pull some weeds.

4

I need a hoe.

10

I see some plants!

I get some <u>seeds</u>.

I plant ______________________ .

I see ________________________ .

Text Copyright © Babs Bell Hajdusiewicz

6

I make a row.

12

I read my little book of nouns to:

1. ______________________________

2. ______________________________

3. ______________________________

I See Numbers

I see numbers on the oven.

2

This book belongs to

______________________________.

Today is ____________________.

8

I see numbers on the key.

I see numbers on the mailbox.

I see numbers on the stapler.

4

I see numbers on the clock.

10

I see numbers on me!

I see numbers on the keyboard.

I see numbers on the ________________.

I see numbers on the block.

I read my little book of nouns to:

1. ______________________

2. ______________________

3. ______________________

Boxes and Boxes

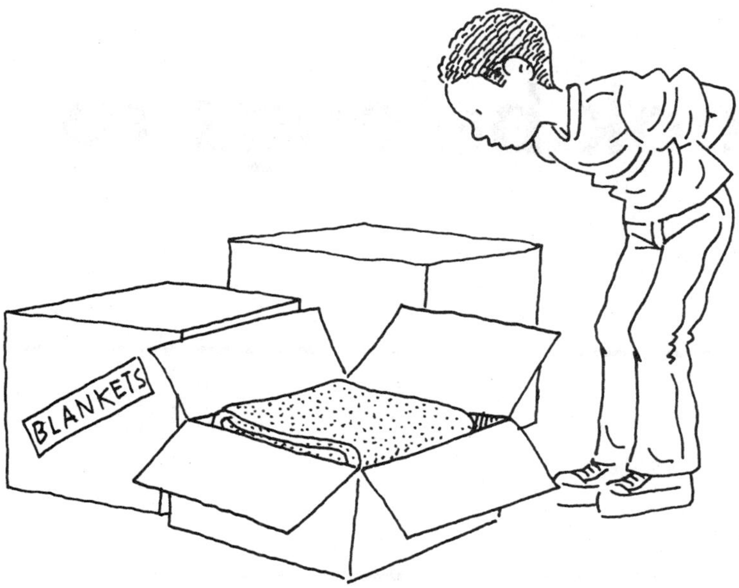

I see boxes on a truck.

2

This book belongs to

______________________.

Today is ______________.

8

I see boxes in the hall.

I see boxes full of dishes.

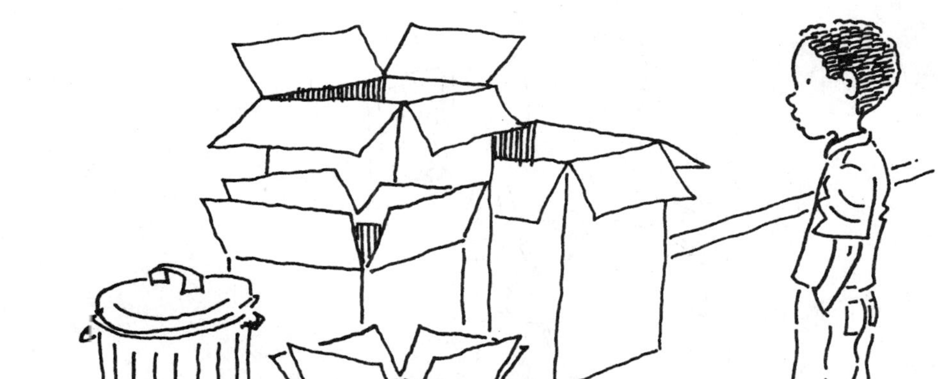

I see boxes in the trash.

4

I see boxes full of clothes.

Text Copyright © Babs Bell Hajdusiewicz

10

I see pictures on the wall.

I see boxes full of blankets.

I have boxes of __________ .

6

I see boxes all in rows.

12

I read my little book of nouns to:

1. ______________________

2. ______________________

3. ______________________

Workers

This worker will clean my teeth.

2

This book belongs to

________________________.

Today is ________________.

8

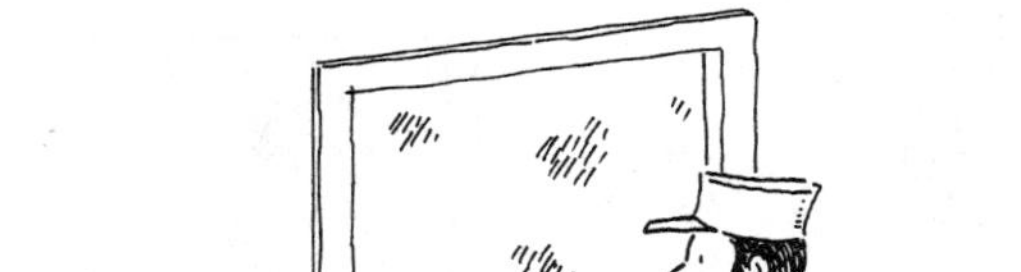

This worker will paint the door.

This worker will bring the mail.

This worker will count the money.

4

This worker will fix the street.

10

This worker will sweep the floor.

This worker will bring the paper.

This worker will __________ the ______________.

6

This worker will weigh the meat.

12

I read my little book of nouns to:

1. ______________________

2. ______________________

3. ______________________

I See Words

I see words on my toothpaste.

2

This book belongs to

______________________________.

Today is ____________________.

8

I see words on my floor.

I see words on my nightshirt.

I see words on my pillow.

4

I see words on my socks.

10

I see words on my door!

I see words on my basket.

I see words on
my ____________.

6

I see words on my box.

12

I read my little book of nouns to:

1. ______________________________

2. ______________________________

3. ______________________________

Text Copyright © Babs Bell Hajdusiewicz

legs	lips
hands	hips
fingers	toes
knees	nose
body	

park	zoo
circus	sister
movies	stores
playground	outdoors
places	

checkers	cats
soccer	hats
flowers	cars
stories	stars
things	

tacos	beans
crackers	greens
pretzels	peas
carrots	cheese
lunch	

elephants	seals
jugglers	wheels
acrobats	clowns
lions	frowns
circus	

baker	typist
painter	clerk
artist	teacher
student	work
jobs	

day	name
time	game
card	place
door	face
party	

pencils	paper
noses	ears
markers	crayons
posters	cheers
school	

hamster	frog
turtle	dog
hippo	bat
lion	cat
pet	

dirt	hoe
seeds	row
water	ants
weeds	plants
plants	

mailbox	clock
keyboard	block
oven	key
stapler	numbers

dishes	clothes
blankets	rows
truck	hall
trash	pictures
wall	boxes

mail	street
paper	meat
teeth	door
money	floor
worker	workers

nightshirt	socks
basket	box
toothpaste	floor
pillow	door
words	